JOHN MERRILL'S PEAK DISTRICT CHALLENGE WALK

Happy walking!
John N. Merrill

ABOUT JOHN N. MERRILL

John combines the characteristics and strength of a mountain climber with the stamina, and athletic capabilities of a marathon runner. In this respect he is unique and has to his credit a whole string of remarkable long walks. He is without question the world's leading marathon walker.

Over the last ten years he has walked more than 55,000 miles and successfully completed ten walks of at least 1,000 miles or more.

His six walks in Britain are—
- Hebridean Journey ....1,003 miles
- Northern Isles Journey ....913 miles
- Irish Island Journey..1,578 miles
- Parkland Journey ....2,043 miles
- Lands End to John O'Groats...................................1,608 miles

and in 1978 he became the first person (permanent Guinness Book Of Records entry) to walk the entire coastline of Britain—6,824 miles in ten months.

In Europe he has walked across Austria (712 miles), hiked the Tour of Mont Blanc and GR20 in Corsica as training! In 1982 he walked across Europe—2,806 miles in 107 days—crossing seven countries, the Swiss and French Alps and the complete Pyrennean chain—the hardest and longest mountain walk in Europe.

In America he used the world's longest footpath—The Appalachian Trail (2,200 miles) as a training walk. The following year he walked from Mexico to Canada in record time—118 days for 2,700 miles.

During the summer of 1984, John set off from Virginia Beach on the Atlantic coast, and walked 4,226 miles without a rest day, across the width of America to San Francisco and the Pacific Ocean. This walk is unquestionably his greatest achievement, being, in modern history, the longest, hardest crossing of the USA in the shortest time—under six months (177 days). The direct distance is 2,800 miles.

Between major walks John is out training in his own area —the Peak District National Park. As well as walking in other areas of Britain and in Europe he has been trekking in the Himalayas four times. He lectures extensively and is author of more than sixty books.

JOHN MERRILL'S PEAK DISTRICT CHALLENGE WALK

by
JOHN N. MERRILL

Maps and Photographs by John N. Merrill

A J.N.M. PUBLICATION

1986

A J.N.M. PUBLICATION

J.N.M. PUBLICATIONS, WINSTER, MATLOCK, DERBYSHIRE, DE4 2DQ.

This book is copyright under the Berne Convention. All rights are reserved. Apart from any fair dealing for the purposes of private study, research, criticism or review, as permitted under the Copyright Act, 1956, no part of this publication may be reproduced, stored in a retrieval system, or transmitted in any other form by any means, electronic, electrical, chemical, mechanical, optical, photocopying, recording or otherwise, without the prior permission of the copyright owner. Enquiries should be addressed to the publishers.

Conceived, edited, typeset and designed by John N. Merrill

© Text and route — John N. Merrill 1986

© Maps and Photographs — John N. Merrill 1986

First published 1983 Reprinted 1984 and 1985 This revised and enlarged edition — September 1986

ISBN No. 0 907496 43 1

Typesetting interfaced by:
Steve Rothwell Typesetting Services, 20 St. Ann's Square, Manchester

fount: Kabel
point size: Headings 16 point text 11 point
line space: 12 point

Printed by:
DESA Ltd., Forest Mills, Alfreton Road, Nottingham NG7 3JL.
Telephone: (0602) 781741.

CONTENTS

INTRODUCTION	1
HOW TO DO IT	2
BAKEWELL TO ROWSLEY—5 Miles	4
ROWSLEY TO ROBIN HOOD'S STRIDE—4 Miles	8
ROBIN HOOD'S STRIDE TO MONYASH—6 Miles	12
MONYASH TO MONSAL DALE—5 Miles	14
MONSAL DALE TO BAKEWELL—5 Miles	18
AMENITIES GUIDE	19
INNS, Y.H.A.'S, B. & B	20
LOG	21
TRAIL PROFILE	22
OTHER BOOKS BY JOHN MERRILL	23
BADGE ORDER FORM	26

VIEW FROM CALLING LOW—LATHKILL DALE IN CENTRE—CALES DALE ON LEFT

INTRODUCTION

The fine traditional market town of Bakewell is the central point of the Peak District, and a logical starting point for a challenge walk in the area. My aim has been to create—
1. a circular walk, using footpaths as much as possible.
2. a walk that could be accomplished within a day—10 hours.
3. a challenge, making the route as rugged as possible, but one that is within everyone's capability.
4. to combine as much scenic variety in the route as possible.

Bearing these points in mind, the walk takes you through limestone scenery—plateaux and dales; across gritstone moorland and past rocky outcrops; and along river valleys. The paths are in the main little used ones. Several of the well-known areas such as Monsal Dale will be seen from different angles providing stunning views. En route are numerous historical sites and ancient monuments. You pass through several villages where there are shops and inns to 'help you' on your way.

I first walked the route over three mornings just before Christmas in appalling conditions—wind, cold and rain. As I walked I checked the route, making careful notes. I have since walked it seven times—usually in eight hours—and can assure you that it is a splendid circuit!

By the end of 1985 more than 3,500 people have completed the walk in an average time of 10 hours. The longest on record is 16 hours, and the fastest—running—is 4 hrs 14 minutes; this was their third attempt! Many have used the walk to raise money for charity, and so far approximately £55,000 has been raised.

All that remains for me to say is—have a good walk, let me know how you get on, and may the sun shine all day and may your feet remain dry and blister free!

Happy walking!

John N. Merrill

JOHN N. MERRILL Derbyshire. 1986

HOW TO DO IT

The whole route is covered by the Ordnance Survey maps — 1:25,000 Outdoor Leisure Map — The White Peak 1:50,000 Sheet No. 119 — Buxton, Matlock and Dovedale

The walk is devised to be done in a single day, allowing between 8-10 hours. There is no criterion to walk it in a day — it is not a competition — and if you want to spend a weekend over it, that's fine. There are hostels, bed and breakfasts, hotels and campsites on or very close to the route to allow you to do this. For those who complete it a four colour embroidered badge and completion certificate is available from JNM Publications.

The route has been carefully mapped with walking notes, and you should have no difficulty walking round. However, during the course of time stiles change, gates change colour and signs disappear. At the time of publication the maps and notes are correct.

Bakewell Town Centre & Starting Point

- ↑ BASLOW
- BRIDGE STREET
- CAR PARK
- INFORMATION CENTRE
- CAR PARK
- RUTLAND SQUARE
- CHEMIST
- INTERNATIONAL STORE
- ← A6 - BUXTON
- → A6 - MATLOCK
- RUTLAND ARMS HOTEL
- BAKEWELL FOR BOOKS
- KING STREET
- ↓ MONYASH

Bakewell to Rowsley—5 Miles

MONSAL TRAIL—One of three disused railway lines in the National Park, now transformed into pedestrian ways. This one, opened in 1981, stretches for 8 miles, from Bakewell to Chee Dale, and was formerly the line from Matlock to Buxton.

BALLCROSS—Former packhorse way to Sheffield and Chesterfield through the steep wood. In 1678 it was paved at a cost of £3.19.8d. (£3.98p). The stone was later removed to build the present road, in 1810. The cross and base have long since been lost.

RUSSIAN COTTAGE—Built like a log cabin, with intricately carved window frames and gable ends. Originally built for a visit by a Russian Czar, it is now a gamekeeper's cottage.

BAKEWELL TO ROWSLEY—5 Miles

River Wye to River Derwent

WALKING INSTRUCTIONS

From Rutland Square walk out of Bakewell along Bridge Street, past the Information Office and across the Wye Bridge. Bear right and ascend Station Road. At the entrance to the small factory complex, turn right up the minor road towards the Golf Course and cross the 'Monsal Trail'. Opposite Elmhurst House, as footpath signposted, turn right and ascend the wide track through the golf course and woodland to Ballcross.

Turn right at the top as signposted and follow the walled track towards Rowsley. Continue along a grass track to a stile on the immediate right of a large pond. Go through a gate beyond and cross the open pastures of Calton Pastures to join a track on the immediate left of a plantation. At the track junction near Russian Cottage, turn sharp right and descend the track, first to Calton Houses and on to Calton Lees, a mile away.

On gaining the road turn right, and, where the road bears right 300 yards later, turn left, as footpath signed, and follow the path to Rowsley, 2 miles away. Cross the first field to a wooden stile on your left, before descending to the valley floor and the River Derwent. Follow the well-stiled path along the valley to Rowsley, entering the outskirts after passing underneath a railway arch. Turn left along the road to the Peacock Hotel, A6 and the centre of Rowsley.

BAKEWELL

A fine old market town on the banks of the River Wye, crossed by a 14th Century five-arched bridge—one of the oldest in the country. The town is the administrative centre of the National Park, and the Market Hall is an Information Centre. There are many old buildings rich in history and legend.

Avenel Court—on King Street; dates from mediaeval times and is close to the old Town Hall and Courtroom built in 1602 by Sir John Manners.

Parish Church—dedicated to All Saints; dates from Norman times. The Vernon Chapel includes the tombs of Dorothy Vernon and Sir John Manners who, in the 16th Century, eloped from nearby Haddon Hall—one of the most romantic legends of the Peak District.

The Rutland Arms—where Jane Austen stayed, and which is featured in her novel 'Pride and Prejudice'. It was the cook at the Rutland Arms who, in about 1859, misunderstood her instructions and made the now famous Bakewell Puddings. They are still made to the original recipe.

RUTLAND ARMS HOTEL, BAKEWELL

RIVER WYE—BAKEWELL

PEACOCK HOTEL, ROWSLEY

Rowsley to Robin Hood's Stride—4 Miles

Thornhills of Stanton in Peak in 1832 to commemorate the passing of the first Reform Bill. The stone with the coronet, large Y and date 1826 commemorates the renowned Duke of York.

BIRCHOVER—Gritstone village famed for its quarries, whose stone has been used in many notable buildings. Close to the Druid Inn is Rowter Rocks, where rooms, passageways, stairs and armchairs have been carved. At first believed to have been the work of the Druids, but now known to be the eccentric work of a member of the Eyre family. Several of the stones are rockable.

Just down the lane from the inn is a small 18th Century chapel built by Thomas Eyre in 1717. In the porch is a plaque to Joan Waste who, believed to be a heretic, was burnt to death in the Windmill Pit, Derby, on August 1st 1556.

ROWSLEY TO ROBIN HOOD'S STRIDE
—4 Miles

River Valley to gritstone outcrops.

WALKING INSTRUCTIONS

Cross the A6 road and walk along School Lane. Just after crossing the River Wye, turn left along the farm road; signposted to Stanton Lees, 2 miles. ¾ mile later, at the drive entrance to Stanton Woodhouse, turn sharp right and follow the twisting farm road around the house and past the farm. Pass through two metal gates and continue ascending on a grass track lined with gorse. Just beyond a large wooden gate the track forks; keep to the left, passing a deep fenced quarry on your left. Gain the minor road via a small wooden gate. Turn right, and at the road junction beyond turn left, signposted for Stanton in Peak.

300 yards up here turn left, as footpath signposted, and follow the path onto Stanton Moor. Ascend the first field on a faint path to the plantation wall, where there is a small stone stile. Enter the wood and gain a well-defined path. In time this merges into the main path on the moor. Continue ahead to the Earl Grey Tower. ¼ mile later, at a wooden stile, bear right and follow the wide path down to the road. Turn right and walk along the level road before descending into Birchover village. Keep the Druid Inn on your right as you descend a narrow lane past the chapel and back into the fields. Where the farm track turns sharp left, keep straight ahead on the path to a stile. Just past a ruined barn, descend to the road. Bear left along it before turning right at the road junction and following the signposted path to Robin Hood's Stride.

PEACOCK HOTEL, ROWSLEY—Built in the 17th Century, the porch lintel bears the date 1652, and a peacock is on top of the turret above. The peacock is the crest of the Manners family—the Dukes of Rutland, owners of nearby Haddon Hall. The inn was originally built as a private residence by John Stevenson, 'man of affairs' to Grace, Lady Manners. The school bearing her name, in Bakewell, was founded by her in 1636.

STANTON WOODHOUSE—Former early 17th Century shooting lodge of the Dukes of Rutland, now a private house. When the Duke of Rutland was restoring his ancestral home—Haddon Hall—early this century, he used the house as his base.

STANTON MOOR—Exceptional viewpoint over the Derwent Valley and Matlock. The heather and bilberry gritstone moorland has several ancient monuments, including a Bronze Age stone circle known as the Nine Ladies; and over seventy burial mounds of the beaker folk have been identified. Finds from excavations can be seen in Weston Park Museum, Sheffield. The Earl Grey Tower on the eastern side was built by the

DOORWAY LINTEL — PEACOCK HOTEL, ROWSLEY

RED LION INN — BIRCHOVER

JOHN MERRILL AT ROBIN HOOD'S STRIDE

Robin Hood's Stride to Monyash—6 Miles

YOULGREAVE—Limestone village dominated by the 15th Century perpendicular tower of the Parish Church. Inside is a unique font incorporating a holy water stoup; a 12th Century monument to Sir John Rossington who holds a heart; and an alabaster panel to Robert Gilbert and family. The church was one of the few to have an 'official dog whipper'. In 1716 he was paid 7p annually to whip the dogs out of the church before divine service. Derbyshire's unique well-dressing ceremony takes place here in June.

ONE ASH GRANGE—Formerly associated with Roche Abbey near Maltby in South Yorkshire. To here misbehaven monks were sent for punishment. A barn has been converted to a camping barn.

ROBIN HOOD'S STRIDE TO MONYASH
—6 Miles
Gritstone outcrops to limestone plateau

WALKING INSTRUCTIONS

Ascend the track towards Robin Hood's Stride, keeping straight ahead where the track turns right to the cottage beneath Cratcliffe Tor. Keep the Stride on your left as you reach the top and cross the fields, using the stiles to 'Cliff Land'. Walk towards Harthill Moor Farm before bearing left around the building and descending to the footpath junction at the bottom of the field. Turn right, and a field later turn left along an ascending track before beginning the descent to the River Bradford. The path is defined in places and well-stiled to Bleakley Dike and on to Bradford.

Turn right at the road, and almost immediately left, along a walled path to the clapper bridge. Cross and turn left, and walk beside the River Bradford to the next clapper bridge. Don't cross it, but keep to the right-hand side of the river and begin ascending the tarmaced railed and stepped path to Youlgreave. At the road, almost opposite the Methodist Church, turn left and follow the road, keeping right at the Middleton junction. Just round the next corner on your right is the path sign and stile. Ascend the field to the next stile before curving right to Moor Lane car park and picnic tables. Turn left at the road, and at the junction 100 yards away cross the road and follow the well-stiled and marked path with yellow-topped posts across the fields to the wood and Calling Low Farm. Walk through the farm yard and descend the fields to Cales Dale, reached by a steep final descent.

Cross the dale floor and ascend to One Ash Grange, passing the farm on its righthand side. Continue along the farm track and, where it curves right, keep straight ahead with the limestone wall on your left. In due course ascend a stile on your left and descend to the shallow Fern Dale. On the other side join a walled track which you follow to Monyash. At the road—Rakes Road—keep straight ahead to the village green and cross.

ROBIN HOOD'S STRIDE—Two gritstone towers whose distance apart—22 yards—is said to be the length of Robin Hood's stride. The rocks provide pleasant scrambling, and are often called 'Mock Beggars' Hall', for the pinnacles look like chamineys. Opposite is Cratcliffe Tor, a popular rock climbing outcrop. At its base is a hermit's cave with a crucifix carved in the 14th Century. On the 'moor' beyond the rocks is a Bronze Age stone circle with four upright stones—the tallest in the Peak District. Castle Ring is the remains of an Iron Age fort.

Monyash to Monsal Dale—5 Miles

FLAGG—situated on the limestone plateau 1,000 ft. above sea level. Annual Point to Point races organised by the High Peak Hunt are held here at Easter. The 16th Century Hall is renowned for its ghosts, and has a skull which, if moved, causes unexplained happenings to occur. The name Flagg means a place where turf was dug for fires.

TADDINGTON—Limestone village whose 18th Century charm has been saved by the bypass. The church is largely 14th Century, with a magnificent 16th Century brass to the Blackwell family and their eleven children. The 18th Century Hall is one of the very attractive smaller impressive buildings of Derbyshire. Like Flagg Hall, ghost stories still linger. At one time a farmer owned the Hall, and every Monday rode to Bakewell Market. He always returned drunk, and one night he walked into the house without opening the door. He is said to still haunt the building.

MONYASH TO MONSAL DALE—5 Miles
across the limestone plateau

WALKING INSTRUCTIONS

From the green, walk along Chapel Street for 75 yards and turn left at the car park; follow the footpath-signed path across the fields to the lefthand side of the row of houses, skirting round the last one to a stile. The path to Flagg is very well-stiled, first to a walled track which you follow to just past a barn on your left. Cross further fields, keeping Knotlow Farm on your right. Beyond, gain the farm track and follow this to the road, which you walk along into Flagg. Cross the main road and walk up the farm road with the Hall on your immediate right. Keep straight ahead through the farmyard to the gate and track. Keep on this and cross the field beyond to the stile and Flagg path sign. Turn right, and left almost immediately, and ascend the stile; walk in the field immediately on the left of a coal merchant's. The path beyond is faint, but all the stiles are there as you pass close to a barn on your right before ascending slightly and curving to the road junction and Taddington road sign.

Descend the road and take the first walled track on your right. As you near the houses, turn right and follow the walled grass track around the buildings before descending to the eastern edge of Taddington village at East View Cottage. Turn right along the No Through Road. ¼ mile along here turn left along a walled grass track and gain the lane to Lodley View Farm. Keep to the left track here and descend to Taddington Field Farm. Turn right and left almost immediately, and descend the shallow dale before curving left to White Lodge car park, picnic tables and A6 road ½ mile away.

MONYASH—Former lead mining centre of the High Peak with its own Barmote Court for settling local mining disputes. The market cross on the green dates back to 1340, and an annual market is still held there in August. The church dates from the 12th Century.

HOBBIT INN—MONYASH

CRATCLIFFE TOR

MARKET CROSS—MONYASH

HOLME BRIDGE, BAKEWELL

BAKEWELL—VICTORIA MILL WHEEL

Monsal Dale to Bakewell—5 Miles

HOLME BRIDGE—Built in 1664 for use by pack-horse teams—hence the low parapet. Upstream is Lumford Mill, a former 18th Century spinning mill where 300 people worked.

VICTORIA MILL—Late 18th Century corn mill in use until 1945. The water wheel has been removed and is adjacent to the building; it measures 16 ft. in diameter by 13 ft. 6 ins. wide.

17

MONSAL DALE TO BAKEWELL—5 Miles
Hilly route back to Bakewell

WALKING INSTRUCTIONS

Cross the A6 road and follow the path across a small stream before turning left and ascending the path to Brushfield. In the early part there are numerous steps to ascend. Gain the farm road via a stile. At the entrance to the farm turn left, as signposted, and walk round the lefthand side of the buildings to the farm track. Follow this to the path-signed junction. Here turn right—'Monsal Dale, Trail and Upperdale'. The path is a walled track for much of its length. As you descend, keep to the righthand track and gain the railway viaduct—the Monsal Trail. Cross the viaduct and ascend to your left to Monsal Head.

Descend the road to Little Longstone. Just past the Packhorse Inn, turn right and, as signposted, cross the fields to Great Longstone. Keep straight ahead along a tarmaced path to the recreation ground. Cross this to Edge View Drive. Walk along this road to its end, and on the right of Charnwood House is the path across the fields to the railway bridge and road junction. Pass under the bridge and turn left along the road to Rowdale House. Turn right on the path, and after the first field ascend through Cracknowl Wood to the fields and Crackendale House. Keep the house on your right to gain a metal kissing gate. Ascend the gentle field beyond. Just over the brow is the stile and the descent to Bakewell. Descend the track to Holme Hall on your immediate left. Cross Holme Bridge and turn left along the A6 road—Buxton Road—back to Rutland Square.

MONSAL HEAD—Perhaps the finest viewpoint in Derbyshire. Down to the perfect curvature of Monsal Dale, with its 120 feet high railway viaduct, now part of the Monsal Trail. The view up the Wye Valley to Cressbrook is particularly attractive. On the river are coots, moorhens, mallard ducks and occasional kingfishers. The dale is rich in flora—monkey flower, butter and the early spring flowers of lesser celandines, cowslips and wood anemones.

GREAT LONGSTONE—Attractive limestone village with small green and cross. Longstone Hall, a classical styled red-brick building, dates from 1747. The church is partly 13th Century, with an exceptionally well-preserved 15th Century nave roof with moulded beams.

HOLME HALL—Beautiful Tudor building with mullioned windows; built in 1626.

AMENITIES GUIDE

Village/Town	B&B	YHA Hostel	Camp-site	Inn	Rest-aurant	Shop	P.O.	Transport (Bus)
BAKEWELL	*	*		*	*	*	*	*
ROWSLEY	*			*	*	*	*	*
BIRCHOVER	*		*	*	*	*	*	*
ELTON (¾ mile off route)		*	*	*	*	*		
YOULGREAVE	*	*		*	*	*	*	*
MONYASH	*		*	*		*	*	*
FLAGG				*				*
TADDINGTON				*		*	*	*
MONSAL HEAD	*			*	*	*		*
LITTLE LONGSTONE				*				*
GREAT LONGSTONE	*			*		*	*	*

INNS

ROWSLEY	GROUSE AND CLARET INN
BIRCHOVER	DRUID INN
	RED LION INN
MONYASH	HOBBIT INN
FLAGG	PLOUGH INN
TADDINGTON	QUEEN'S ARMS INN
MONSAL HEAD	MONSAL HEAD HOTEL
LITTLE LONGSTONE	PACKHORSE INN

Y.H.A.

BAKEWELL	FLY HILL — Tel. Bakewell (062981) 2313
YOULGREAVE	FOUNTAIN SQUARE
	Tel. Youlgreave (062986) 518

ELTON   THE OLD HALL — Tel. Winster (062988) 394

BED AND BREAKFAST

BAKEWELL	Milford House Hotel, Mill Street, Bakewell, DE4 1DA. Telephone: Bakewell 2130
	Mrs. K.H. Pheasey, Bourne House, The Park, Bakewell. Telephone: Bakewell 3274
ROWSLEY	Peacock Hotel, Rowsley Telephone: Darley Dale 3518
BIRCHOVER	Mrs. C. Hobbs, Brickfields Cottage, Eagle Tor, Birchover. Telephone: Winster 459
	Mrs C.V. Kelsey, Rocking Stone Farm, Birchover, Derbyshire. Telephone: Winster 356
YOULGREAVE	M. Shimwell, Church Farm, Youlgreave, DE4 1US. Telephone: Youlgreave 305
	The Bulls Head Hotel, Youlgreave, Bakewell, Derbyshire. Telephone: Youlgreave 307
MONYASH	Lea Hurst, Monyash. Telephone: Bakewell 2575
	The Hobbit Inn, Monyash, Bakewell. Telephone: Bakewell 2372
MONSAL HEAD	Castle Cliffe Private Hotel, DE4 1NL Telephone: Great Longstone 258
	Merlin House, Ashford Lane, DE4 1NL. Telephone: Great Longstone 475
	Monsal Head Hotel Telephone: Great Longstone 250
GREAT LONGSTONE	Mrs. R. McGoverne, Willow Croft, Station Road, Great Longstone. Telephone: Great Longstone 576
CAMPING BARN	A converted barn to a hut type accommodation, with bed space and cooking facilities. Only one on the route at — One Ash Grange, above Cales Dales. Details and bookings to — Peak National Park Study Centre, Losehill Hall, Castleton, Derbyshire, S30 2WB.

LOG

DATE...................... TIME STARTED..................... TIME COMPLETED......................

Route Point	Mile No	Time Arr.	Time Dep.	Comments/ Weather
Bakewell—Rutland Square	0			
Ballcross	1			
Calton Pastures	1½			
Calton Houses	2¼			
Calton Lees	3¼			
Rowsley—A6	4¾			
Stanton Woodhouse Farm	5¾			
Stanton Moor—Tower	6¾			
Birchover—Red Lion	8			
Robin Hood's Stride	9			
Harthill Moor Farm	9¼			
River Bradford	10¼			
Moor Lane Car Park	11¾			
Calling Low	12¾			
One Ash Grange Farm	13½			
Fern Dale	14¼			
Monyash—Cross	15			
Flagg	16½			
High Well—Taddington	18			
Taddington Field	19			
A6 Road	19½			
Brushfield Hough	20			
River Wye	21			
Monsal Head	21½			
Little Longstone	22			
Great Longstone	22½			
Rowdale House	23			
Crackendale House	23¾			
Holme Hall	24¼			
Bakewell—Rutland Square	25			

TRAIL PROFILE—3,600 ft. of ascent

22

OTHER BOOKS BY JOHN N. MERRILL & PUBLISHED BY JNM PUBLICATIONS

DAY WALK GUIDES

SHORT CIRCULAR WALKS IN THE PEAK DISTRICT Fifteen carefully selected walks—3 to 5 miles—starting from a car park. The walks cover the variety of the area—the gritstone edges, limestone dales, and peat moorland. All follow well defined paths; include a pub for lunch; and are suitable for all the family. 44 pages 16 maps 22 photographs   ISBN 0 907496 37 7

PEAK DISTRICT TOWN WALKS Twelve short circular walks around the principal towns and villages of the Peak District. Including Castleton, Buxton, Hathersage, Eyam, Tissington and Ashbourne. Each walk has a detailed map and extensive historical notes complete with pictures. 60 pages 12 maps 96 photographs   ISBN 0 907496 20 2

PEAK DISTRICT: LONG CIRCULAR WALKS Fifteen differing walks 12 to 18 miles long for the serious hiker. Many follow lesser used paths in the popular areas, giving a different perspective to familiar landmarks. 64 pages 16 maps 28 photographs   ISBN 0 907496 17 2

WESTERN PEAKLAND—CIRCULAR WALKS The first book to cover this remarkably attractive side of the National Park—west of Buxton. The guide combines both long and short walks. 25—3 to 11 mile long walks with extremely detailed maps to help you explore the area. 48 pages 23 maps 22 photographs   ISBN 0 907496 15 6

12 SHORT CIRCULAR WALKS AROUND MATLOCK 12 walks of about 4 miles long into the Matlock area rich in history and folklore and make ideal family outings. Included is an 'alpine' walk, using Matlock Bath's cable car as part of the route. 52 pages 44 photographs 12 maps   ISBN 0 907496 25 3

SHORT CIRCULAR WALKS IN THE DUKERIES More than 25 walks in the Nottinghamshire/Sherwood Forest area, past many of the historic buildings that make up the Dukeries area. 56 pages 40 photographs 21 maps   ISBN 0 907496 29 6

CANAL WALKS VOL.1—DERBYSHIRE AND NOTTINGHAMSHIRE More than 30 walks both short and long along the canals in the area—Cromford, Erewash, Chesterfield, Derby, Trent & Mersey, Nottingham, Beeston and Nutbrook canals. 84 pages 60 photographs 32 maps   ISBN 0 907496 30 X

HIKE TO BE FIT...STROLLING WITH JOHN John Merrill's personal guide to walking in the countryside to keep fit and healthy. He describes what equipment to use, where to go, how to map read, use a compass and what to do about blisters! 36 pages 23 photos 2 sketches 3 charts   ISBN 0 907496 19 9

CHALLENGE WALKS

JOHN MERRILL'S PEAK DISTRICT CHALLENGE WALK A 25 mile circular walk from Bakewell, across valleys and heights involving 3,700 feet of ascent. More than 2,000 people have already completed the walk. A badge and completion certificate is available to those who complete. 32 pages 18 photographs 9 maps   ISBN 0 907496 18 0

JOHN MERRILL'S YORKSHIRE DALES CHALLENGE WALK A 23 mile circular walk from Kettlewell in the heart of the Dales. The route combines mountain, moorlands, limestone country and dale walking with 3,600 feet of ascent. A badge and certificate is available to those who complete the route. 32 pages 16 photographs 8 maps   ISBN 0 907496 28 8

JOHN MERRILL'S NORTH YORKSHIRE MOORS CHALLENGE WALK A 24 mile circular walk from Goathland in the heart of the moors. The route combines moorland, river valley and coastal walking and uses Robin Hood's Bay as the half way point. Involves 2,000 feet of ascent and a badge and certificate is available to those who complete. 32 pages 18 photographs 9 maps   ISBN 0 907496 36 9

THE RIVER'S WAY A two day walk of 43 miles, down the length of the Peak District National Park. Inaugurated and created by John, the walk starts at Edale, the end of the Pennine Way, and ends at Ilam. Numerous hostels, campgrounds, B&B, and pubs lie on the route, as you follow the five main river systems of the Peak—Noe, Derwent, Wye, Dove, and Manifold. 52 pages 35 photographs 7 maps   ISBN 0 907496 08 3

PEAK DISTRICT: HIGH LEVEL ROUTE A hard 90 mile, weeks walk, around the Peak District, starting from Matlock. As the title implies the walk keeps to high ground while illustrating the dramatic landscape of the Peak District. The walk was inaugurated and created by John and is used by him for training for his major walks! 60 pages 31 photographs 13 maps   ISBN 0 907496 10 5

PEAK DISTRICT MARATHONS The first reference book to gather together all the major and classical long walks of the Peak District between 25 and 50 miles long. Many are challenge walks with badges and completion cards for those who complete. The longest walk—280 miles—inaugurated by John is around the entire Derbyshire boundary. Each walk has a general map, accommodation list, and details of what guides and maps are needed. 56 pages 20 photographs 20 maps   ISBN 0 907496 13 X

HISTORICAL GUIDES

WINSTER—A VISITOR'S GUIDE A detailed look at a former lead mining community which still retains a Morris dancing team and annual pancake races. A two mile walk brings you to many historical buildings including the 17th century Market House. Illustrated by old photographs. 20 pages 21 photographs 1 map
         ISBN 0 907496 21 0

DERBYSHIRE INNS The first book to tell the story behind more than 150 inns in the Peak District and Derbyshire area. With details of legends, murders and historical anecdotes, the book gives added pleasure or impetus to explore the pubs of the region. Profusely illustrated with 65 photographs and a brief history of brewing in Derbyshire. 68 pages 57 photographs 5 maps   ISBN 0 907496 11 3

100 HALLS AND CASTLES OF THE PEAK DISTRICT AND DERBYSHIRE A visitor's guide to the principal historical buildings of the region. Many are open to the public and the guide describes the history of the building from the Domesday Book to the present time. The book is illustrated by 120 photographs and makes an excellent souvenir gift of one of England's finest architectural areas. 120 pages 116 photographs 4 maps   ISBN 0 907496 23 7

TOURING THE PEAK DISTRICT AND DERBYSHIRE Twenty circular routes of about 50 miles for the motorist or cyclist. Each route has a set theme, such as the gritstone edges or in the steps of Mary, Queen of Scots. Deatiled maps for each route and fifty photographs make this a useful companion to the Peak District/Derbyshire area. 76 pages 45 photographs 20 maps   ISBN 0 907496 22 9

JOHN'S MARATHON WALKS

EMERALD COAST WALK The story of John's walk up the total length of the west coast of Ireland and exploration of more than fifty islands—1,600 miles. 132 pages 32 photographs 12 maps
         ISBN 0 907496 02 4

TURN RIGHT AT LAND'S END In 1978 John Merrill became the first person to walk the entire coastline of Britain—6,824 miles in ten months. The book details the route, how he ascended our three major mountains and how he found a wife. Included are more than 200 photographs he took on the walk, which is also a unique guide to our coastline. 246 pages 214 photographs 10 maps   ISBN 0 907496 24 5

WITH MUSTARD ON MY BACK John has gathered together the stories of his first decade of walking—1970-1980. Here is a collection of unique walks in Britain, from a 2,000 mile walk linking the ten National Parks of England and Wales together to a 450 mile walk from Norwich to Durham.
         ISBN 0 907496 27 X

TURN RIGHT AT DEATH VALLEY During the summer of 1984, John walked coast to coast across America, a distance of 4,226 miles in 177 days. Few have walked across and none have taken so difficult a route. He crossed all the main mountain ranges, climbed 14,000 foot mountains, crossed deserts in 100 degrees, walked rim to rim of the Grand Canyon in 8½ hours, and crossed the famed Death Valley. The walk is without parallel and the story is the remarkable tale of this unique adventure. ISBN 0 907496 26 1

FORTHCOMING TITLES—

SHORT CIRCULAR WALKS IN THE STAFFORDSHIRE MOORLANDS
ARKWRIGHT OF CROMFORD
CANAL WALKS VOL.2—DERBYSHIRE, CHESHIRE AND STAFFORDSHIRE
CANAL WALKS VOL.3—DERBYSHIRE, LEICESTERSHIRE AND LINCOLNSHIRE
THE LITTLE JOHN CHALLENGE WALK

EQUIPMENT NOTES—some personal thoughts

BOOTS—preferably with a leather upper, of medium weight, with a vibram sole. I always add a foam cushioned insole to help cushion the base of my feet.

SOCKS—I generally wear two thick pairs as this helps to minimise blisters. The inner pair of loop stitch variety and approximately 80% wool. The outer a thick rib pair of approximately 80% wool.

WATERPROOFS—for general walking I wear a T shirt or shirt with a cotton wind jacket on top. You generate heat as you walk and I prefer to layer my clothes to avoid getting too hot. Depending on the season will dictate how many layers you wear. In soft rain I just use my wind jacket for I know it quickly dries out. In heavy downpours I slip on a neoprene lined cagoule, and although hot and clammy it does keep me reasonably dry. Only in extreme conditions will I don overtrousers, much preferring to get wet and feel comfortable.

FOOD—as I walk I carry bars of chocolate, for they provide instant energy and are light to carry. In winter a flask of hot coffee is welcome. I never carry water and find no hardship from doing so, but this is a personal matter. From experience I find the more I drink the more I want. You should always carry some extra food such as Kendal Mint Cake for emergencies.

RUCKSACK—for day walking I use a climbing rucksac of about 40 litre capacity and although excess space it does mean that the sac is well padded and with a shoulder strap. Inside apart from the basics for the day I carry gloves, balaclava, spare pullover and a pair of socks.

MAP & COMPASS—when I am walking I always have the relevant map—usually 1:25,000 scale—open in my hand. This enables me to constantly check that I am walking the right way. In case of bad weather I carry a Silva type compass, which once mastered gives you complete confidence in thick cloud or mist.

PEAK CHALLENGE

Badges are yellow cloth with figure embroidered in four colours and measure — 3" wide x 3½" high.

BADGE ORDER FORM

Date completed..
Time..
Name...
Address ....
....
....

Price: £1.75 each, including VAT, postage and completion certificate.

GET A JOHN MERRILL WALK BADGE—complete this walk twice or another of his challenge walks. The badges are circular and four coloured embroidered. Send details and £1.75 to JNM Publications.

From: JNM Publications, Winster, Matlock, Derbyshire, DE4 2DQ.
Telephone: Winster (062988) 454.

REMEMBER AND OBSERVE
THE COUNTRY CODE

ENJOY THE COUNTRYSIDE AND RESPECT ITS LIFE AND WORK.

GUARD AGAINST ALL RISK OF FIRE.

FASTEN ALL GATES.

KEEP YOUR DOGS UNDER CLOSE CONTROL.

KEEP TO PUBLIC PATHS ACROSS FARMLAND.

USE GATES AND STILES TO CROSS FENCES, HEDGES AND WALLS.

LEAVE LIVESTOCK, CROPS AND MACHINERY ALONE.

TAKE YOUR LITTER HOME—PACK IT IN, PACK IT OUT.

HELP TO KEEP ALL WATER CLEAN.

PROTECT WILDLIFE, PLANTS AND TREES.

TAKE SPECIAL CARE ON COUNTRY ROADS.

MAKE NO UNNECESSARY NOISE.